This adventures belongs to:

_____

_____

_____

_____

_____

_____

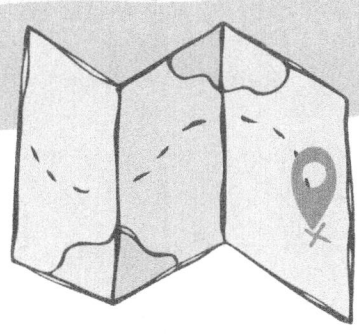

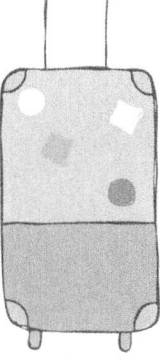

120 Exciting Bucket List Ideas for inspiration

1   See the Eight World Wonders.

2   Orgasm at the same time.

3   Ride a horse on the beach.

4   Visit all the continents in the world.

5   Stay in an overwater bungalow.

6   Rent a beach house for the whole summer.

7   Go scuba diving.

8   Buy a homeless person a full meal.

9   Travel to a place or country you have never been together.

10 Go parasailing

11 Take a road trip

12 Make food and pass it out to the homeless.

13 Design your own house and build it.

14 Complete an obstacle race: Spartan, Tough Mudder, Zombie Mud Run, etc.

15 Float in the Dead Sea.

16 Attend a class or workshop: cooking, art, glass blowing, chocolate making, etc.

17 See the Hobbit town in New Zealand.

18 Spend the night at the ice hotel in Quebec.

19 Experience 24 hours of daylight in Alaska.

20 Hike the 54 fourteeners in Colorado.

120 Exciting Bucket List Ideas for inspiration

21   Go backpacking through Europe.

22   Become financially independent.

23   Have sex somewhere new. E.g. On a boat.

24   Attend a wine tasting.

25   Have a couple's book club.

26   RV across a country.

27   Visit an ancient city.

28   Ride in a hot air balloon.

29   Have sex outside.

30   Read the same books and discuss.

31   Build an orphanage or school.

32   Go on a gondola ride in Venice.

33   See the eiffel tower in Paris.

34   Bobsled in Prague.

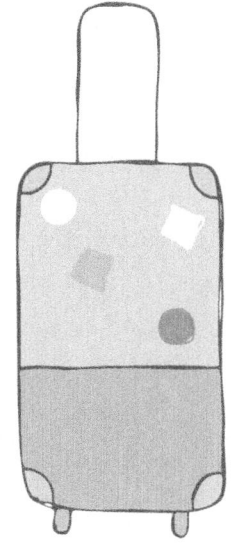

35   See the northern light in Finland.

36   Experience paradise in Maldives.

37   Experience oktoberfest in Germany.

38   Have a memorable first kiss.

39   Plan a trip to somewhere you've never been.

40   Watch each other's favorite movies.

120 Exciting Bucket List Ideas for inspiration

41   Go on an adventure.

42   Go on a double date.

43   Play 20 questions.

44   Stay up all night talking.

45   Have a tech-free date together.

46   Kiss in the rain.

47   Plan our future.

48   Say "I love you."

49   Have our song.

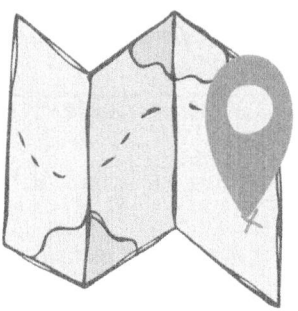

50   Go backpacking through Europe.

51   Go skinny dipping together.

52   Take our picture in a photo booth.

53   Meet each other's families.

54   Watch the sunset.

55   Watch the sunrise.

56   Tell each other our secrets.

57   Binge watch a new TV series.

58   Go to the theatre.

59   Attend a wedding together.

60   Have brunch together.

120 Exciting Bucket List Ideas for inspiration

61   Live in a different country.

62   Stay in bed all day.

63   Share our true feelings.

64   Sing a karaoke duet.

65   Start a new tradition together.

66   Slow dance.

67   Get tattoos together.

68   Get engaged.

69   Kiss under the stars.

70   Go to a midnight movie.

71   Take a road trip together.

72   Become regulars somewhere we love.

73   Take a brewery tour.

74   Cook dinner together.

75   Read the same book (at the same time).

76   Build a pillow fort.

77   Have a picnic.

78   Write each other love letters.

79   Dine out at an upscale restaurant.

80   Have sex on the beach.

120 Exciting Bucket List Ideas for inspiration

81 Go to a museum together.

82 Kiss underneath fireworks.

83 Dress up in a couples costume for Halloween.

84 Make a relationship playlist.

85 Make out at the drive-in theatre.

86 Ride around town on a motorcycle.

87 Go camping together.

88 Get married.

89 Take a honeymoon.

90 Go to a wine tasting.

91 Spend a day at a spa.

92 Join the mile high club.

93 Play mini golf.

94 Make a relationship time capsule.

95 Go bowling.

96 Wear matching sweaters for holiday cards.

97 Take a long walk on the beach.

98 Buy a home together.

99 Go for a hike.

100 Take a bubble bath together.

120 Exciting Bucket List Ideas for inspiration

101	Host a couples game night.
102	Go ice skating.
103	Get flowers just because.
104	Kiss on top of a ferris wheel.
105	Celebrate our anniversary.
106	Fly first class.
107	Have a baby.
108	Host a dinner party.
109	Learn ballroom dancing.
110	Have breakfast in bed.
111	Rent a beach house for a summer.
112	Go sailing.
113	Recreate our first date.
114	Volunteer together.
115	Take a food tour.
116	Ride on a tandem bicycle.
117	Adopt a shelter pet.
118	Stay in an over-water bungalow.
119	Add a love lock to a bridge.
120	Relax together in a hot tub.

Our Bucket List

Page

Our Bucket List

Our Bucket List

1

We did it

When:

Where:

Our Memories:

What we learned:

We did it

When:

Where:

Our Memories:

What we learned:

3

We did it

When:

Where:

Our Memories:

What we learned:

_____

4

We did it

When:

Where:

Our Memories:

What we learned:

5

We did it

When:

Where:

Our Memories:

What we learned:

We did it

When:

Where:

Our Memories:

What we learned:

7

We did it

When:

Where:

Our Memories:

What we learned:

_____

_____

_____

We did it

When:

Where:

Our Memories:

What we learned:

9

We did it

When:

Where:

Our Memories:

What we learned:

_____

We did it

When:

Where:

Our Memories:

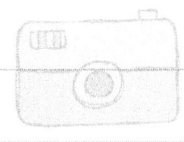

What we learned:

11

We did it

When:

Where:

Our Memories:

What we learned:

We did it

When: _____

Where: _____

Our Memories: _____

_____

_____

What we learned: _____

_____

_____

13

We did it

When:

Where:

Our Memories:

What we learned:

We did it

When:

Where:

Our Memories:

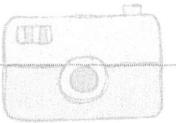

What we learned:

15

We did it

When:

Where:

Our Memories:

What we learned:

We did it

When:

Where:

Our Memories:

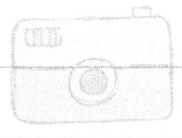

What we learned:

17

We did it

When:

Where:

Our Memories:

What we learned:

We did it

When:

Where:

Our Memories:

What we learned:

19

We did it

When:

Where:

Our Memories:

What we learned:

_____

_____

_____

We did it

When: _____

Where: _____

Our Memories: _____

_____

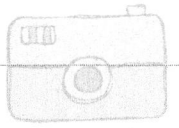

_____

What we learned: _____

_____

_____

21

We did it

When:

Where:

Our Memories:

What we learned:

We did it

When:

Where:

Our Memories:

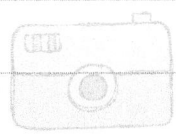

What we learned:

23

We did it

When:

Where:

Our Memories:

What we learned:

We did it

When:

Where:

Our Memories:

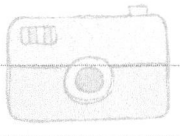

What we learned:

25

We did it

When:

Where:

Our Memories:

What we learned:

We did it

When:

Where:

Our Memories:

What we learned:

27

We did it

When:

Where:

Our Memories:

What we learned:

We did it

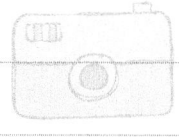

When:

Where:

Our Memories:

What we learned:

29

We did it

When:

Where:

Our Memories:

What we learned:

We did it

When:

Where:

Our Memories:

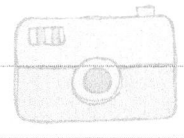

What we learned:

31

We did it

When:

Where:

Our Memories:

What we learned:

We did it

When:

Where:

Our Memories:

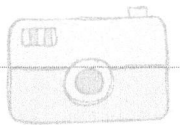

What we learned:

33

We did it

When:

Where:

Our Memories:

What we learned:

We did it

When:

Where:

Our Memories:

What we learned:

35

We did it

When:

Where:

Our Memories:

What we learned:

_____

_____

We did it

When: _____

Where: _____

Our Memories: _____

_____

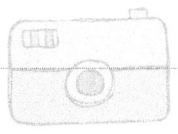

_____

What we learned: _____

_____

_____

We did it

When:

Where:

Our Memories:

What we learned:

We did it

When:

Where:

Our Memories:

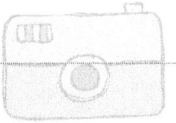

What we learned:

39

We did it

When:

Where:

Our Memories:

What we learned:

_____

_____

_____

We did it

When: _____

Where: _____

Our Memories: _____

_____

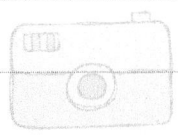

_____

What we learned: _____

_____

_____

41

We did it

When:

Where:

Our Memories:

What we learned:

We did it

When:

Where:

Our Memories:

What we learned:

43

We did it

When:

Where:

Our Memories:

What we learned:

We did it

When:

Where:

Our Memories:

What we learned:

45

We did it

When:

Where:

Our Memories:

What we learned:

_____

_____

_____

We did it

When: _____

Where: _____

Our Memories: _____

_____

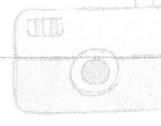

What we learned: _____

_____

_____

We did it

When:

Where:

Our Memories:

What we learned:

We did it

When:

Where:

Our Memories:

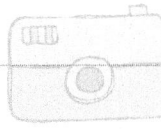

What we learned:

49

We did it

When:

Where:

Our Memories:

What we learned:

We did it

When:

Where:

Our Memories:

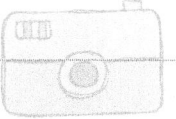

What we learned:

51

We did it

When:

Where:

Our Memories:

What we learned:

_____

We did it

When: _____

Where: _____

Our Memories: _____

_____

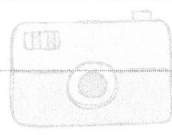

_____

What we learned: _____

_____

_____

53

We did it

When:

Where:

Our Memories:

What we learned:

_____

54

We did it

When:

Where:

Our Memories:

What we learned:

55

We did it

When:

Where:

Our Memories:

What we learned:

We did it

When:

Where:

Our Memories:

What we learned:

We did it

When:

Where:

Our Memories:

What we learned:

We did it

When:

Where:

Our Memories:

What we learned:

59

We did it

When:

Where:

Our Memories:

What we learned:

We did it

When:

Where:

Our Memories:

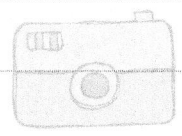

What we learned:

61

We did it

When:

Where:

Our Memories:

What we learned:

We did it

When:

Where:

Our Memories:

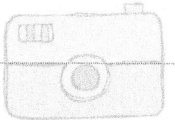

What we learned:

63

We did it

When:

Where:

Our Memories:

What we learned:

We did it

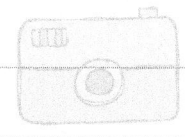

When:

Where:

Our Memories:

What we learned:

65

We did it

When:

Where:

Our Memories:

What we learned:

We did it

When:

Where:

Our Memories:

What we learned:

We did it

When:

Where:

Our Memories:

What we learned:

....

....

....

We did it

When:

Where:

Our Memories:

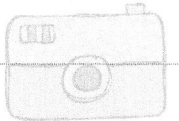

What we learned:

69

We did it

When:

Where:

Our Memories:

What we learned:

We did it

When:

Where:

Our Memories:

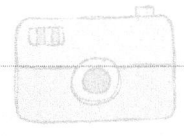

What we learned:

71

We did it

When:

Where:

Our Memories:

What we learned:

We did it

When:

Where:

Our Memories:

What we learned:

73

We did it

When:

Where:

Our Memories:

What we learned:

We did it

When:

Where:

Our Memories:

What we learned:

75

We did it

When:

Where:

Our Memories:

What we learned:

We did it

When:

Where:

Our Memories:

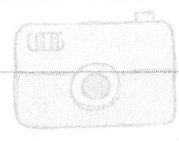

What we learned:

We did it

When:

Where:

Our Memories:

What we learned:

We did it

When:

Where:

Our Memories:

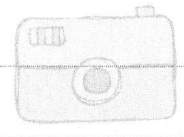

What we learned:

We did it

When:

Where:

Our Memories:

What we learned:

We did it

When: ....

Where: ....

Our Memories: ....

....

....

What we learned: ....

....

....

81

We did it

When:

Where:

Our Memories:

What we learned:

We did it

When:

Where:

Our Memories:

What we learned:

83

We did it

When:

Where:

Our Memories:

What we learned:

We did it

When:

Where:

Our Memories:

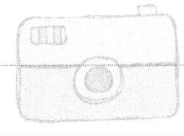

What we learned:

85

We did it

When:

Where:

Our Memories:

What we learned:

We did it

When:

Where:

Our Memories:

What we learned:

87

We did it

When:

Where:

Our Memories:

What we learned:

We did it

When:

Where:

Our Memories:

What we learned:

We did it

When:

Where:

Our Memories:

What we learned:

We did it

When:

Where:

Our Memories:

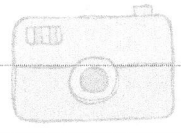

What we learned:

91

We did it

When:

Where:

Our Memories:

What we learned:

We did it

When:

Where:

Our Memories:

What we learned:

93

We did it

When:

Where:

Our Memories:

What we learned:

We did it

When:

Where:

Our Memories:

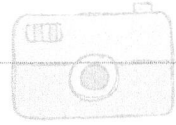

What we learned:

95

We did it

When:

Where:

Our Memories:

What we learned:

We did it

When:

Where:

Our Memories:

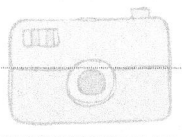

What we learned:

We did it

When:

Where:

Our Memories:

What we learned:

We did it

When:

Where:

Our Memories:

What we learned:

99

We did it

When:

Where:

Our Memories:

What we learned:

We did it

When:

Where:

Our Memories:

What we learned:

Special Notes:

Special Notes:

Special Notes:

Printed in Great Britain
by Amazon